THE LAST VISIT

This book is dedicated to the late Ian R. Beaton B.V.M.S., M.R.C.V.S.

If it wasn't for him giving me my very first job, and paying for my Diploma, I wouldn't be where I am today. Thank you, Mr Beaton.

THE LAST VISIT

Cycle Counselling is a Pet Bereavement Counselling Service owned and managed by Carrie Ball, a Veterinary Care Assistant, and Pet Bereavement Counsellor.

Innovet-CPD is a Veterinary Training provider. Vicki Stout is the Managing Director.

Contact Us Phone:

07522202498

Email:
cyclecounselling@hotmail.com

Innovet-CPD.

Email: www.innovet-cpd.co.uk

Phone: 01942 207610
07914 064370

Special thanks must be given to:

My parents, my sister Ellen, and my fiancé Paul. They all believed I could. So, I did.

Vicki Stout, thank you for giving me the chance to enable staff to assist clients at such a sensitive time.

I would also like to thank Compassion Understood, Luke Fisher and colleagues,

THE LAST VISIT

for allowing me to use quotes from your webinar.

01788 228811

info@compassionunderstood.com

I would like to also thank Mike Davies from www.provet.co.uk. **who kindly allowed me to use a quote from their website.**

THE LAST VISIT

Cycle Counselling was created after many years working in veterinary practice. I became a Companion Animal Bereavement Counsellor in 2001. Since then I have qualified as a VCA, gained a Diploma in animal behaviour, a Level 3 certificate in Pet Bereavement, a Certificate in Counselling Skills, and a certificate for completion of The Client Journey from Compassion Understood.

I had seen many a client sent away with the bare minimum of support. A leaflet for the crematorium, a scrap of paper with a number for the Blue Cross Bereavement line. I wanted to be the one to provide a service like no other. Yes, there are other pet bereavement counsellors out there. But, not everyone has the background and knowledge I have. I have the advantage of being from the other side of the consulting table. I have first-hand experience of many years 'down the back'. This book and the CPD course provided by and lead by Vicki Stout of Innovet CPD, co-written and tutored by myself, will go a long way to enabling staff to help their clients.

THE LAST VISIT

The last visit doesn't have to be the last visit. This book will tell you how.

**THE LAST VISIT**

CONTENTS.

Chapter 1.

**End of life doesn't mean end of commitment.**

Chapter 2.

**End of life consults.**

Chapter 3.

**Different types of client.**

Chapter 4.

**Little things can make a BIG difference.**

Chapter 5.

How the client can help in the last days.

Chapter 6.

What to say and what not to say.

Chapter 7.

Stages of grief.

Chapter 8.

Types of grief and their meanings.

Chapter 1.

End of life doesn't mean end of commitment.

Most of the pets we meet are first brought in for primary vaccinations. We may see them throughout their whole lives for one reason or another. Sometimes we meet pets that are older and have a story to tell.

No matter why or when a pet is brought in to us, we must be aware that our commitment begins as soon as that client opens the door. But our commitment doesn't necessarily end when they leave.

THE LAST VISIT

Throughout the life of that pet we are asked to assist when it is ill, injured or needs routine examinations or vaccinations. We care for the pet, and in turn we provide support to the owner. The reason the owner comes back, and seeks us when their pet needs veterinary attention, is because we care, and we are always there.

When the pet is nearing the end of its life, or is chronically or terminally ill, or injured beyond help, we do not stop caring, and we do not stop giving support.

The client will have gotten to know the staff to some degree, we all have those clients that we consider friends in a way, and the ones we

THE LAST VISIT

would do anything for (within reason).

The client comes to the surgery because we all want the same thing, what is best for that pet. The client trusts us, and our judgement, and that is why end of life care is so important.

When the pet dies or we must perform euthanasia, the client is looking to us for that support. In a way, the client looks to us as if we too are losing as much as they are and feeling as badly as they are.

The client expects us to be aware of the depth of their loss. We as a practice have been through so much with this pet, and when it dies there is no reason for us to metaphorically wash our hands of it. Our work is far from over.

Once that pet has died, the owner will still look to the staff for support. The owner will be needing that back up that they have had since day one.

One of the many things I learned whilst working in veterinary practice, is that there is a need for support of clients that have suffered a loss.

I saw my first euthanasia when I was 18 years old. The experience stayed with me for a long time. I wrote a blog about it entitled Dear Little Brown Dog.

THE LAST VISIT

If you feel so inclined, you can read it below. Dear Little Brown Dog,

Hi, you won't remember me, but I will never forget you. We first met 16 years ago, at Mr B's Veterinary Clinic.

You had been brought in by your loving owner, and little did either of us know, but this was going to be one of THOSE consults.

Your owner spoke to Mr B, explained what you had been doing symptom wise, and what she had brought you in for. I was stood near the dispensary door, a sliding door in gloss finish, thick white paint, that had been on for years, shelves upon shelves of drugs and

THE LAST VISIT

bottles lined those shelves, I only tell you this because I was suddenly VERY interested in the paint work when I heard WHY you had been brought in. "Put to sleep", aw sounds lovely, a nice long sleep that you weren't expecting. I was 18, naïve, young, and innocent. Looking for a job working with animals.

Stroking them, cuddling them, walking them, feeding them.

Till I realised that sometimes we must kill them. That's the long and short of it. Euthanasia means "gentle death", we give patients that need it a gentle passing, a way out of the pain and distress, or we put an end to the potential for pain

THE LAST VISIT

and distress in the future, that can't be stopped by medication.

So, sorry Little Brown Dog. Back to you. So, I heard the words, had no idea what they meant. Then the elastic band came out, and the artery forceps, and the curved scissors and the meth swab. The needles and a large brown bottle of liquid from the locked cupboard. The liquid was drawn up in the syringe, and I was still unaware.

The fur was clipped from your right front leg (I think it was right). J the nurse held you as Mr B wrapped the elastic band round your leg and used the artery forceps to clamp it tight. The swab wiped the

THE LAST VISIT

bare skin. Then the hush descended.

The needle went in, blood came back when the plunger was drawn back, and my world was changed in an instant.

As the liquid entered your blood stream, your legs buckled, (God, I can barely type here, I am back in that room), you slowly laid down on the table, and I am ashamed to say, I screamed, I sobbed I was hysterical. I was ushered into the dispensary and I sat on the kick stool and a piece of my heart died with you.

THE LAST VISIT

You had died!!! This little brown dog that had been stood on the table a minute ago, was now dead.

Something in me died that day, my very first euthanasia. J tried to comfort me, the owner was asking about me too. "How is that girl?" "is she ok?" "Yes, she will be fine, first time you know?" "oh, ok. Never gets easier, does it?". "Never gets easier, does it?". I have heard this a lot over the years, no, it doesn't get easier, at all, but we learn to cope.

Little brown dog, that day you died, you ignited something in me, I decided that from that day on I would do whatever it took to make sure no one felt as bad as I did that day. I wanted to be there with a hug, a brew, and a shoulder to cry on or words of comfort.

Thanks to you I have set up my own Counselling service, helping people where I can. Little Brown Dog, the day you died, you gave me the push to start LIVING.

Thank you.

Good night.

Writing that, I was back in that room. I remember it all so vividly. There were many more euthanasia's after that one over the years, some of them are forever with me.

THE LAST VISIT

 I made it my personal duty to ensure that no owner felt that no one cared, that no one understood.

 I asked Mr Beaton (now sadly passed away), about a course I had seen advertised. It was with the Animal Care College and was a Diploma in Companion Animal Bereavement Counselling. At the time, it was about £30 I think, and I was so happy, this was the course for me. I wanted to do it so badly.

 Mr Beaton was used to me having all sorts of ideas and whims and he said he would pay for it, but I had to keep at it and work hard.

THE LAST VISIT

I was over the moon, and applied straight away. I completed the course and passed and the passion for this subject has only grown over time.

I worked for Mr Beaton for 10 years as his sole employee. I assisted him with many euthanasia's and would like to think that I helped a lot of owners.

When Mr Beaton retired, I was employed within an animal hospital. I made it clear through opinion and actions, that pet bereavement was my 'thing' and I was keen to help anyone I could.

THE LAST VISIT

I was usually the auxiliary called upon to see to a client that had just lost their pet.

The one that escorted a hysterical owner from the premises and made sure they were ok. I was the one that memorised the caskets and other options available for cremation. The one who wrote the cards for the plaque and rang owners of DOA patients identified by a microchip. I was the one that made sure that the patients looked presentable when the owners came to view them.

The one who cleaned and dressed the RTA victim so the owner would not see the extent of the injuries. The one who rang owners to make

THE LAST VISIT

sure they had gotten home ok, and the one that made a brew and got a chair for those too distressed to even think.

My colleagues were great, they too put a lot of effort into assisting clients, they too did all the above but I felt it was my area, the aspect of veterinary practice in which I could make a difference.

What surprised me was that some clients were sent away with the bare minimum of support. A leaflet for the crematorium at most. A phone number for the Blue Cross. One lady that I was asked to see to showed me the need for more support in practice.

THE LAST VISIT

The lady had a cat, which had been euthanized. She was very close to this cat and was heartbroken.

The lady had taken the cat back home so she could have one more night with him before he was sent to the crematorium. However, this lady did not know that she could have taken her cat to the crematorium herself. She did not know that she could make an appointment, and wait and collect the ashes straightaway.

When I explained this to her, she was shocked and so grateful. I was surprised she hadn't been told and had had to go through all the pain of bringing her beloved cat back to the surgery.

I must admit I was irritated. That she had gone through all this needlessly. With just a little fact finding by the practice, she could have had all the options available and made the best decision for her.

I was surprised at the number of clients that did not know the options for burial, or cremation. That there were several options for the ashes and they could be tailored to suit the client. I.e. a scatter pouch is lovely for keeping in a beautiful box or to be planted under a bush or plant. A scatter tube is perfect for scattering the ashes on a favourite walk.

THE LAST VISIT

A tribute box has a section on top for a favourite photo.

A casket came in Beech, Mahogany or paw print urn. The plaque could be personalised.

Many a time I spent trying to fit a personal message onto the request slip. Making sure as best I could that all the words the owner wanted were placed just so. It wasn't seen as a chore, or a nuisance. It was the least we could do to lessen the pain and ensure the owner got the tribute they wanted.

THE LAST VISIT

This book is written with a view to helping you to help clients.

It is written by someone that has seen their fair share of loss, angry clients, hysterical clients, and heartbroken clients.

At the end of reading this book, I would hope that you, the reader, have a better understanding of what the client may be thinking.

How they may be feeling and how we as professionals can ensure that the last visit is not the 'last'.

Chapter 2.

End of life consults.

Can you remember your first euthanasia? Can you recall your first DOA? How did you feel? Did you put your professional head on and just do what had to be done?

What about afterwards? How did you feel on your break? Did the past event come to mind, or did you not give it a second thought because you knew what to expect, what happens and why?

We see so much, the injuries that have our vets reaching for the pentobarb. The patients that crash and no matter how hard we try they cannot be saved.

We are trained for pretty much any event. We know what to expect. We anticipate it, and we are ready.

As veterinary staff, we know what happens during and after euthanasia.

We know why a patient may need sedation, and we know how this may affect the pet. We know that a pet may not have great blood pressure, and so may need a catheter, or to receive the final injection in their kidney or heart.

We know that small furries and birds are usually anaesthetised via gas such as Iso or Sevo before euthanasia. We know that when the pet dies it may gasp, empty its bladder and or bowels, and may stretch.

We know that the 'gasp' is the diaphragm relaxing as the brain is finally starved of all oxygen.

We know that the pet may exhibit an excitation stage and appear to be struggling and fighting for life. We know that when the ashes come back they may feel lighter or heavier than expected.

What is important to remember here is that the owner may not know all the above. This is what leads to added stress and fear.

THE LAST VISIT

Think back to the very first time you saw a patient die. Think back to how you felt, how you felt *before* you fully understood the how's and why's.

Now imagine how the client may feel. Imagine seeing it for the very first time, imagine not having the knowledge that we do.

It is the knowledge that keeps our professional persona in place, the reason we can take a step back and deal with the pup that crashed after the section. The reason we can place the RTA cat into the body bag. The reason we can do the job we do.

THE LAST VISIT

We need to give the clients enough time to process the information, and give them all the relevant information they need.

'46% of vets discuss end-of-life care with pet owners on more than 11 occasions per month

70% of vets felt further training in pet loss would be beneficial

20 to 25% of pet owners change vets after pet bereavement'.
Compassion Understood.
Compassion Understood Pet Loss Vets.

https://www.compassionunderstood.com. [Accessed 8 October 2017].

THE LAST VISIT

It is the unknown that can lead to misunderstandings and a very dissatisfied and distraught client.

We are so frightened of upsetting clients by even mentioning euthanasia and the loss of their pet. Unfortunately, by not even talking about it till the time has arrived, we are in danger of making our clients very distressed and even angry.

We have nurse clinics for everything from worming, vaccination, and puppy socialisation etc. It seems appropriate to assist clients by preparing them for unexpected events and the expected loss.

THE LAST VISIT

A handout is also a great way to allow clients to have all the information they need, and they can read it when they can. The client is also more likely to take in the information. On the handout, there would be the most asked or thought of questions, or questions answered that a vet would want the client to know. The handout would also ideally include phone numbers of either pet loss support sites like The Ralph Site (who also have a list of pet bereavement counsellors), Compassion Understood or the Blue Cross. Even a number for local Pet Bereavement Counsellors or the Samaritans. The Samaritans are not just there for when someone is contemplating ending their life.

The clinic and or handout show the client that we understand.

There would ideally be a list of options available to the client regarding cremation. This would include prices for cremation and ashes and choice of casket.

This allows the client time to process the information and decide when they are not in an overly emotional state.

There are a few types of grief which will be explained in more detail in Chapter 6. There is a type that is named disenfranchised grief. There are some losses that are taboo almost, some losses that the grieving person cannot talk openly about for fear of ridicule or because they feel that their loss is invalid.

I have heard so many people apologise for their feelings because they do not think that their loss is worthy of grieving for. How many times have you heard or seen someone say, "I'm sorry for being so upset, it was only a ......"?

Or "I don't know why I am so sad, it was only a fish etc. ....".

The person tries to validate their feelings, or explain their feelings to someone else in a way that is almost asking the other person to accept or at least validate their feelings. The bereaved person is almost anticipating that the other person will not understand their loss.

This leads to the person pushing back their feelings, and if the person they are opening to is not accepting of their feelings, they will be further convinced that their loss and grief doesn't matter. This is sad; we have no right to say what size or type of pet deserves grieving over. Only the owner can decide how they choose to react to the loss.

No matter the size of pet, only the owner knows the depth of the love and the amount of loss felt.

THE LAST VISIT

As veterinary staff, it is important that we do not fall into the trap of disenfranchised grief.

By not approaching the subject of pet loss, and not supporting or informing the owner about the ins and outs, we are at risk of contributing to and cementing the belief that the loss is not worth the grief.

52% of pet owners said that they would have welcomed information on normal feelings around pet loss and stages of grief. (Compassion Understood)

52% is a lot of clients that have been left with no prior knowledge of what may happen, and how this may affect them.

This figure is mainly due to staff being scared to mention the D word. We must not forget that death is one of the few things in this life that is a certainty. We and the clients know this, but shouldn't they also know what happens, why we choose euthanasia, what that means, and what support is out there for end of life?

We have SOP'S for most aspects of the surgery. So why do we not have a S.O.P for end of life?

There are many standard operating procedures in veterinary practice. From anything to deep cleaning a ward to wrapping a kit. They are there to show staff how something should be done ideally.

A uniform instruction set for all staff, so that everyone knows how to do a task. And even if they have never done it before, or aren't feeling confident about it, the SOP shows them exactly how it is done.

''From Wikipedia, the free encyclopaedia

A standard operating procedure, or SOP, is a set of step-by-step instructions compiled by an organization to help workers carry out routine operations. SOPs aim to achieve efficiency, quality output, and uniformity of performance, while reducing miscommunication and failure to comply with industry regulations."

In most practices, there is that one member of staff who the other staff members and clients go to when upset. The member of staff that shows sympathy, says, and does all the right things. The one who 'gets' it. But what happens when that staff member is off sick, or on holiday?

Having a bereavement SOP means that not only can most if not all staff look after a bereaved client, but that the level of care is uniform and exceptional.

It also takes the pressure off the staff who find it difficult to assist clients when showing outward signs of discomfort.

So, when is a good time to discuss end of life?

There may be differing opinions on this, when is the time right?

Some people would disagree that the topic of end of life should be discussed while the pet is still healthy and very much alive. Some people may think that this discussion should take place if the pet receives a poor prognosis or when they are getting old.

However, some pets do not live till they are old, some develop life threatening ailments at a young age, some die from tragic accidents, or other unforeseen circumstances.

The owner then must deal with not only the news, but also try to take in the information about what happens before the pet dies, or after.

They are left with a lot of information that could have been given prior. When they were in a clearer frame of mind to process it. This is where euthanasia consults can be so helpful.

A Compassion Understood Survey had the following result "31% of owners say they didn't feel well prepared for their pet's euthanasia appointment".

THE LAST VISIT

An informal clinic would be a good way to broach the subject of end of life, age and age-related issues could also be discussed. It would help the client to be prepared and to have any questions they may have answered.

The client can talk to the vet well before any decision would even be thought of.

The consultation would allow the client to go home with all the relevant information they need and to make a decision that is not rushed and not made in the heat of the moment when emotions are running high.

THE LAST VISIT

The consultation would ideally cover the main topics that cause more grief for the clients. The topics that are not usually covered till the time comes, and the ones that we may not have thought to be an issue.

We should think like a client. I.e. a person that is not familiar with the behind the scenes work of a veterinary practice.

A questionnaire could be created which allowed clients to express what areas they would like more information on. And this in turn

helps the vet and other staff because you are not guessing at what the client wants.

THE LAST VISIT

Topics to include would ideally be:

What happens during a euthanasia consult?

How will I know if the time is right?

Who can attend the final consult?

What happens or may happen when a pet is sedated?

What happens to the pet physically during euthanasia?

What may happen once the pet has died?

What options are there for the pet afterwards?

How much does the procedure cost, and the cremation etc.?

What tribute options are there?

How and when is payment taken?

How long does the process of euthanasia take?

What happens to the pet afterwards?

Topics such as the above are the main areas that clients may need clarification.

The areas that may lead to misunderstandings and awkward conversations at a time when emotions are high.

By covering them in consult when the owner can take in the information, and process it, means less stress later. The practice can also include a fact sheet in the practice welcome packs, or as a standalone fact sheet that clients can collect.

Below is a copy of a leaflet I created for clients.

The Last Goodbye

An owner's guide through the death of a pet.

Euthanasia means 'gentle death'. It is performed when a pet is too ill, injured or elderly to continue.

Quality of life has reduced and the kindest option is to allow our beloved pet to die with dignity and some of their old spark.

This is no doubt a very difficult time; there are so many questions and not enough time.

THE LAST VISIT

This booklet aims to guide you through the euthanasia or unexpected death of your pet,

and hopefully answer your questions and put your mind at rest.

Firstly, we need to look at what euthanasia means.

It is the ending of a pet's life due to injury or illness. It is a humane way of ensuring that they suffer no longer.

<u>Why is there a need to perform euthanasia?</u>

In veterinary practice, there are occasions when a pet has reached the end of its natural life, but to allow it to die naturally would mean possible suffering and would be inhumane. There are times when a pet is so injured that their only respite is euthanasia.

Or illness has become so severe that to continue would be cruel. A veterinary surgeon performs euthanasia; they have reached the decision that this is the only kind option available. We rely on vets to diagnose and treat issues our pets may have, and we trust their judgement is always in the best interests of our pet.

Euthanasia is carried out by injecting a solution into the pet's bloodstream that will stop the heart and allow the pet to die quickly and peacefully.

Euthanasia is the only option left available, so what happens?

The process is aimed to be as relaxed and stress free for all concerned as possible. However, in stressed or fractious animal's sedation may be given to calm the pet. The vet requires access to a vein, ideally in a fore (front) leg, or occasionally a back leg. Sometimes the injection is administered into the heart or a kidney. This depends on the severity of the pet's condition and the vet performing the euthanasia.

If the patient is very ill, it can be difficult to locate a vein if the blood pressure has dropped.

It is in this circumstance that a catheter may be placed to guarantee access. A catheter is a tube of plastic that is inserted into a vein, and allows the introduction of fluids directly into the vein. This minimises the risk of missing the vein, or losing the vein due to reduced blood pressure. Sometimes sedation is used to calm a pet that is scared, stressed, or resents being held.

This may lead to a reduction in blood pressure, so a catheter may

THE LAST VISIT

be required. The vet will proceed to inject the solution.

The pet will lose consciousness rapidly and sometimes before the injection has ended the pet has already passed away.

It is sometimes possible that a pet will 'gasp' or stretch their legs. This could look alarming if you are not prepared and it is not a sign of life, it is merely a sign that the pet has died.

Your pet may pass urine and faeces at the time; this is natural

and is to be expected as the muscles relax.

THE LAST VISIT

Possible reactions to the death of a pet.

Elizabeth Kubler Ross describes grief as a cycle, there are five stages.

The five stages are:

Denial

Anger

Bargaining

Depression

Acceptance.

There is no rule to say which stage we enter first or how long we shall stay in each stage. Our personal situation will determine this.

THE LAST VISIT

Denial: To make this situation easier, we may tell ourselves it isn't really happening. Our minds try to protect us by refusing to acknowledge the fact that our pet is ill, dying or has died.

We may try to refuse what the vet has said, we heard it, but our mind won't allow us to believe it.

It is both ok to feel like this and not to experience this. We are all individual and react differently to bad news. Denial only lasts if we want it to, the more we hang onto this feeling the longer it stays with us. We can't move on until we accept to some degree what has or is going to happen. However, much we want it to, denying the facts will not alter anything.

Anger: This may be directed at ourselves, we may feel angry with ourselves for whatever reason we believe caused the death of our pet. 'Why didn't I do this', 'Why did I do that?' These are the questions we may be asking ourselves.

A life changing decision has been made and we may feel powerless. We may feel we had no say in matters. The outcome may have been sped up or delayed but no matter what nothing we said or did or didn't do would change the outcome.

THE LAST VISIT

We may even feel anger towards our pet for being ill in the first instance, if they had never gotten ill, we would not have to deal with this. It is irrational and deep down we know that it is our mind trying to make sense of the situation. We may try to hold someone else accountable; we may blame a friend who was pet sitting, the kennels, cattery, or the vet. In our minds if we had been there this would never have happened.

If we can blame someone else rather than ourselves, we can feel justified in our reaction.

This is all natural; we are trying to make sense of a situation we felt we had no time to prepare for. There is never enough time, and this can make us feel angry.

Bargaining: This is our way of trying to prolong or delay the inevitable. By trying to stall, when we know there is none left. We may try all manner of ways to gain precious few hours, days, weeks. We may appeal to a higher being, or promise ourselves certain unwritten resolutions. 'If I do this' 'If I promise to do this...'. 'Give me just enough time to...'

There are so many if I's and if I just's. We know that even if by some miracle, we get another day, that it's not going to stop what we know

59

THE LAST VISIT

is coming. We try to deal with the panic, the uneasiness. It makes us feel slightly more in control, however the ending is usually the same.

Depression: We know what needs to be done, or has happened. And life may seem to have lost meaning. We have lost a dear friend and there may be thoughts of 'what's the point?'

There may be occasions where we 'see' or 'hear' our pet.

This is understandable, as we may have shared many months or years together, and suddenly the house is just a bit too quiet. At times when we feel low, we need to reassure ourselves that it is natural, we are bereaved. We must allow ourselves time to adjust and grieve and come to terms with our loss.

Acceptance: A time when we come to terms with our loss that no matter what we say or do nothing is going to change the situation. We can think about and talk about our pet without being too upset.

We can remember the good times, rather than focusing on the last days.

There may be a time when we feel ready for another companion. It may be sooner rather than later or never. It is important to remind ourselves that although we can never replace our lost friend, we can replace what is 'normal' for us, i.e. if we have always had a pet then we may feel that another one fills the void. This is truly a personal decision.

This is a cycle of grief. Each person goes through the cycle to some degree. Some people get stuck on one part; others go through it just to repeat the cycle.

There will always be a trigger, a moment, event, or place that reminds us of what we have lost.

Time is a great healer; it does get easier and a bit less raw.

Remember not who you lost but remember how lucky you were.

THE LAST VISIT

You were lucky because you had the love, fun, joy of owning your pet. It was for you and your family that they purred, chirruped, and wagged their tails.

No one outside your group of family and friends knows how much your pet meant to you. No one apart from you really 'knew' them like you did. Try to hold onto that thought. You gave your pet the best life they could ever have asked for. They and you were lucky to have found each other.

You have your memories and nothing can take them away from you.

THE LAST VISIT

This leaflet was designed to aid clients through the stages of grief, and what happens during and after euthanasia.

This leaflet or similar could be printed and made available to clients.

The consult should be available to any owner, at any stage, and they should be aware that this is available at the practice. This way the owner can make their own decision to attend.

The consult should be as warm and informal as possible without being unprofessional.

Moving the table to the side of the room and arranging the seats so that you can sit and talk to the owners. Having a cup of tea or coffee can give comfort and is an object of warmth that the owner can focus on if the talk gets, too difficult.

Try not to have a table in-between you and the clients as it may be subconsciously seen as a barrier in communication.

Keep the body language open and warm, but bear in mind that the subject is an emotive one and so have tissues ready.

Chapter 3.

Different types of client.

There are different types of client, and different ages and lifestyles and reasons for owning the animals they do. The way we deal with each client varies, and depends on the individual. We tailor the consult to suit the audience as it were.

It is important to keep in mind how the different types of client may react to the loss of a pet, and how best to approach this subject. We would not speak to a child the way we speak to an adult.

THE LAST VISIT

In this chapter I describe the main types of client, and how best to assist them.

Children-

Need to be shielded as much as possible from the negative side of euthanasia and or death- i.e. soiling, muscle spasms, stretches and gasps. This is hard enough for an adult let alone a child.

Discuss with the parents prior to the appointment what they are happy for their children to see.

Have a plan in place to keep the child/ren occupied in case they cannot be present in the consulting room.

THE LAST VISIT

Children react to the loss of a pet in a variety of ways. Depending on the age of the child and their mental emotional age, their understanding of death varies from child to child.

When dealing with the loss of a pet and children, it is important to be honest. Age appropriately honest. However, we need to respect the views of the parents or guardians.

We cannot decide what is best for the child at the time of euthanasia in the practice. However, we can decide if the visit is likely to have an adverse effect, we can advise but that is all we can do.

THE LAST VISIT

If the patient is in a very bad way, i.e. serious injuries or needs sedation which may lead to excitation, then we can advise that the child or children be better off not in the room.

The visit itself should be as calm and child friendly as possible. If possible have a consult room ready, then the family can wait in there with their pet.
When it is time for the euthanasia, have a member of staff take the children into a spare consult room or back into reception.

Sit with them, and talk to them about their day at school for instance or make conversation about tv. The child/ren may not wish to converse, and that is to be expected.

Allow the child to see their pet if the parents agree. Offer them a paw print, a clipping of fur or the pets collar. Listen to them if they decide to open to you.

If you have a grief pack ready, you can give this to them which gives the child something to focus on. A grief pack consists of

1. A card (In this instance my business card)

2. A plant pots

3. A pack of forget me not seeds and thyme seeds.

THE LAST VISIT

4.   A keyring with space at the back to put a favourite photo in.

5.   A candle to light the darkness

6.   A voile bag to hold a fur clipping.

This pack is one that I make for my clients, it is easy to make in bulk and is a nice gesture to a grieving client.

This is a handout that I created for children.

THE BRIGHTEST STAR IN THE SKY

A CHILDRENS GUIDE TO THE LOSS OF A PET

THE LAST VISIT

We love our pets and we never want anything bad to happen to them.

Sometimes though our pets get very poorly or are badly hurt.

When this happens, we do not want them to be in pain. Our parents or guardians take them to the vet to help them.

Sometimes there is nothing the vet can do to make them feel better. You might hear this word

EUTHANASIA

(Youth an a zee a).

This means gentle death. When there is nothing else we can do, the vet performs euthanasia. The vet will talk to you and your family, about what they are going to do. The vet or a nurse will

THE LAST VISIT

Will clip some fur from your pet's front leg and give an injection of a special liquid that is just for very poorly or hurt pets. A nurse will hold your pets leg to help the vet.

You can talk to your pet and stroke them. The vet will inject your pet, this injection means that your pet will die peacefully and quickly.

This might look and sound mean, but it is the kindest thing to do for your pet. We do not want them to hurt anymore.

The vet will warn you that after the injection your pet may make a noise like a gasp or stretch their legs. This can sometimes happen after they have died, but is normal and means they are not alive anymore.

THE LAST VISIT

Sometimes they might have a wee or a poo.

It can be scary to watch sometimes, so do not feel silly if you cannot stay.

It doesn't mean you don't love your pet, they know you love them very much.

It is normal to feel many things afterwards. You might feel angry at your parents, the vet or even yourself, this is ok. It won't last.

You might feel guilty, maybe thinking it was your fault, but you know what? No matter what you said or did it was never your fault.

You might feel jealous because other people have pets and yours has gone. This is ok too, it is natural and normal.

THE LAST VISIT

Remember you can always talk to someone you trust. They won't think you are being silly.

It is normal to cry and not to cry, do whatever feels better. After the vets, you can take your pet home to bury them or leave them at the vets to be cremated.

If you want to remember your pet always, you can make a box filled with their favourite toys in it, and a photo or a piece of fur.

It is a very sad time when a pet dies. We love them so much, and they knew this. No matter what, your pet loved you to bits. Your family will be there for you no matter what. You can even talk to a teacher you trust about how you feel.

THE LAST VISIT

If you need to talk to someone else you can ring the lovely people at Child line 0800 11 11, they will never think you are being silly and will listen to you. Or call the Child Bereavement Trust 0845 357 1000.

Your pet is now the brightest star in the sky.

When you see the stars in the night sky, you can look for the brightest one and blow a kiss and say Goodnight.

Below is an open letter I created for children, it is at the parent's discretion whether they feel it would help or not.

Dear _____,

THE LAST VISIT

Hello! I just wanted to write you a letter to tell you everything I didn't get chance to say.

I love you, I tried to show you in so many ways, and I am sure you knew. But I wanted to tell you that I was so happy with you, the cuddles, and the fussing. And the treats! Oh, the treats were lovely!

I really enjoyed living with you, and being owned by you. You were the BEST owner in the world EVER!

THANK YOU, I LOVE YOU.

THE LAST VISIT

I know it was sad when I had to go, but I am happy again, and I am playing with lots of other pets and we are all the best of friends.

I know I can't see you in person, but please don't be sad, I really am ok, and I will always love you. You can't always see the stars at night, but you know they are still, there, right?

Well it's the same for me, you might not be able to see me, but I am there in your heart and memories. Paint me a picture, write me a letter, blow a kiss to the brightest star in the sky.

I will always be glad that you were my owner.

I LOVE YOU TO THE MOON AND BACK AGAIN.

AND I ALWAYS WILL.

Lots and lots of love and snuggles,

pet name_____

There are several books available which help children through the loss of a pet.

One of my personal favourites is Megan's Journey written by Janet Peel. It tells the tale of Megan, a Westie who passes away and explains what it is like at the 'Rainbow Bridge'.

It is beautifully written and is a wonderful book for children to read, or have the book read to them.

The most important thing to remember, is that the best thing for the child is for them to know the permanence of the loss.

When we use euphemisms, we are only asking for trouble. Phrases such as 'put to sleep', 'gone to live on a farm', 'gone on holiday', or "run away", only lead to the child believing that the pet can come back, or thinking that they did something to make the pet disappear. It is surely harder to see a child pine for a pet that we know will never come back, than to let them grieve and adjust to the loss.

Ways to help a child can include:

Reading a book together such as Megan's Journey by Janet Peel.

Painting a picture of the pet for their wall, or even one for the practice.

Writing a letter to their pet can be helpful, it is surprising how much you get down on paper.

Memory boxes are a lovely way for a child to remember their pet. A simple card box with pens and stickers for the child to decorate themselves. This gives the child some control over a situation in which they have none. They can decorate the box in any way they like, and they can fill it with small items to remind them of their pet.

Another idea is to place a fur clipping in a Build a Bear, this way the child can cuddle the bear and the fur inside.

If the child is struggling to cope, they can call Child Line, or the Blue Cross Helpline. However, in some cases the child may need to speak to a professional counsellor.

Elderly-

This loss may take its toll in a subtle or dramatic way.

THE LAST VISIT

Ensure there is a private room, ample space so as not to be claustrophobic. Offer a glass of water, or offer to call a taxi if needed. Call the client after an hour or so after they should have gotten home, to make sure they are ok.

Call after a couple of days to keep the lines of communication open. This is very important. For some elderly clients, their pet may be their only companion and after the loss they may be going home to an empty house. By calling the client afterwards you are helping them more than you may know, they are aware that there are people out there that care.

THE LAST VISIT

From the client's point of view there may be many reasons why the loss may be felt more. They may be reminded of their own mortality. Morbid as it may sound.

There may be feelings associated with the memories around first acquiring the pet. The circumstances that led to taking on the pet in the first place. Such as maybe the pet was bought after the death of a spouse, or after children had moved out.

The pet would have provided comfort and company at a hard time.

There may be feelings of loss of use or purpose as the pet provided a routine, a reason for getting up in the morning, dressing, eating etc.

It is important to remember that from the client's point of view that they have just lost one of the most important things in their life. The loss may bring back feelings of unresolved grief from other losses experienced.

Offer support, make time for a chat and a cup of tea. Call the client after a couple of days to make sure they are ok.

Put the client in touch with a charity such as the Blue Cross or a pet bereavement counsellor.

Bear in mind also that costs involved with the euthanasia and or cremation may be an issue also, so it may be worth arranging a payment plan that is agreeable with the practice just in case. This means that there is one less stressor for the client.

Disabled client-

Bear in mind the role of the animal. Was this a therapy animal? An assistance dog or a medical alert dog? The role the animal had in that person's life will have an impact on how the loss affects them. Be aware that they have lost an extension of themselves.

THE LAST VISIT

For a disabled client, they have lost so much more than a companion.
For the disabled client, the dog (usually a dog) has been a lifeline, a means of leaving the house because of the emotional support, a way to navigate places and interact with other people. They may not have time to grieve properly before they are assigned a new companion.

There are lots of different types of assistance dogs. Medical alert dogs,

PTSD support, Autism support, Guide Dogs etc.

THE LAST VISIT

Whatever the reason the person has, that dog is a major part of their life. That dog is their link to the outside world, their support, their friend, an extension of themselves.

These dogs provide love, courage, support, and a lifeline in many cases. They perform tasks in the home, they let the handler know when the doorbell goes, they lead and guide, they stay by the handler's side and protect them from themselves. Autism support dogs for instance can be attached to their handler, and if the handler tries to run off the dog is trained to sit and refuse to budge.

THE LAST VISIT

Understanding that the loss is much more than losing a companion is important. The handler 'owner' may feel like they have lost everything, their newfound independence, their confidante.

The owner will be awaiting a new canine partner, there may be not much time to adjust to the loss before receiving a new dog.

There may be issues such as unresolved grief as the loss intermingles with the brief loss of assistance. Be aware that the client may be angry but not necessarily at you. The loss may remind them of what the dog gave to them and this is hard to deal with.

As with all clients, be sympathetic, be the shoulder to cry on or just the ear to listen. Do not be afraid to say the wrong thing, being silent can be just as bad as saying something heartfelt but it being taken the wrong way.

At the end of the day you can only offer your support, and that of other people i.e. Blue Cross or bereavement counsellors. It is ultimately up to the client what they feel would help, but if you offer at least you have shown sympathy and compassion.

Chapter 4.

Little things can make a BIG difference.

As discussed previously, we must always bear in mind that the clients do not have the background that we do, that they do not have the knowledge that we do. We need to ensure that we treat all clients with the respect they deserve, and treat them as we would want to be treated if the roles were reversed.

Please be aware of the circumstances around the death of the pet, or the reason for the euthanasia.

THE LAST VISIT

Try to place yourself in the client's shoes, how might the circumstances affect them? Was the death caused by injury or illness? Was it a sudden death?

Was the loss expected? Were the pet young or old?

Try to plan for all eventualities, prepare in plenty of time so that the practice is ready for the client. Consider who attends the practice at this time, are there children present? Is the client elderly or disabled?

Preparation is the key.

Would it be possible to have a spare consult room dedicated to euthanasia and visits? This may not always be possible, but can save a lot of hassle.

However, making sure a room is available when the client attends for their appointment is helpful. Having the room ready means that when the clients arrive they can be offered privacy. They can have a few moments alone before and after away from the busy waiting room. Offering privacy shows that you respect the client. It shows that you understand how hard this time can be.

So, the time has come, a decision has been made and the client is in the surgery awaiting their appointment. Have a member of staff greet the client as they come into the surgery, and escort the client to the room. Ask the client if they want some time alone, or would they prefer you to stay?

The client is experiencing one of the most devastating times of their life. There are a hundred and one thoughts going through their minds.

 All sorts of emotions from fear, to sadness to the light-headed feeling of adrenaline surging.

Do not leave them to wait in the waiting room.

This may seem obvious, but many a time I have seen a distraught owner sat with their pet, sobbing waiting to go in. In a waiting room, full of cats, barking dogs, and other distractions. This is the worst moment of their life at that time. They are here because they are about to say goodbye to their beloved companion.

The last thing they need is to be surrounded by noise, and other animals that may be there for routine procedures, and other clients that may want to strike up a conversation.

The staff are there to be the strength that the client needs. The client needs reassurance that they are making the right decision, they need to be reminded that they are not being judged and that everyone is understanding.

The client probably feels guilt, sadness, numbness, despair and needs the staff to be the shoulder to cry on, the support in their time of need.

The staff should be respectful, courteous, and think ahead. Once the client has entered the room, it is then up to you to discreetly leave and make sure the client knows where you are when they are ready to leave.

Listen to the client, do not try to speak too soon, do not worry about what to say, just be there. Offer a cup of tea or coffee or a glass of water. a seat in a quiet room. Allow the client time to settle and recover from the shock of what they have experienced.

It is little things that can mean so much to the client. For instance, how do we let other clients know that there is something going on?

Some practices have a flameless candle on the reception desk.

A plaque states that when the candle is lit someone is saying goodbye to a beloved pet. It asks that they show respect, i.e. keeping voices down to a low volume, watching what is said and how it may be perceived. Staff would be aware too and cautious not to talk too loudly, or jovially. There is nothing worse than having someone breaking their heart in the other room, and hearing laughter or what the staff are planning to do over the weekend.

The candle is a subtle way of showing that something important is going on. There are other ways this can be done, be it a sign on the reception desk, to a curtain drawn over the door.

It is surprising what sticks in your mind, how despite what is going on, there are always other things in the background that seep into your subconscious.

THE LAST VISIT

These things may seem insignificant, and they may not be of apparent concern to us. But in the moment, when you are facing saying goodbye to a beloved pet, it is surprising what sticks with you. There may have been a delay in the owner and pet being seen, there may have been a lot of other pets in that day. There may have been staff talking or laughing in the other rooms.

Making sure all staff are aware that there is a euthanasia about to take place is helpful. It means that ALL staff are aware, and react and act accordingly. It is also helpful because it means that the client is expected and they would not have to explain why they are there. I can't think of anything more upsetting.

The fact is that if an owner is not happy with the way their pets end of life was dealt with, they won't always tell you. Clients tend to vote with their feet.

The loss of the client is a 'silent loss', as you may not be aware that they have left. The client may get another pet but may not go back to the original practice.
This may be because the experience was so traumatising that they cannot bear to go back to the same clinic, let alone see the same vet or go in the same room.

THE LAST VISIT

Client attrition may be due to;

1.   The client moves to a new house and the practice is no longer close enough.

2.   The client did not get another pet after the loss

3.   The client could not face going back, even if the euthanasia was well handled.

4.   The client may have had no support and felt that they could not return.

A client moving to a new house, or not taking on another pet is obviously something that we cannot control, but more importantly this decision is not based on our performance at the time of euthanasia or after the loss of a pet.

When preparing for a euthanasia it is important to bear in mind the size of the patient and who will be attending the appointment.

For a large dog, it would be beneficial to move the consulting table (if possible) to the side of the room. Placing incontinence sheets on the floor in the middle of the room and laying bedding on top. Placing sheets underneath means that any bodily fluids are drawn away from the patient and the bedding and won't be obvious to the client.

THE LAST VISIT

The placement of the bedding allows the clients to gather around the pet and make sure that everyone gets to be around the pet. It may be worth having spare vet beds folded to make the client comfortable.

Having a chair available for elderly or infirm clients is also beneficial.

Placing a box of tissues near the bedding allows clients to take a tissue in their own time.

Ensuring the equipment necessary is to hand. Clippers plugged in or fully charged, stethoscope, swabs, spirit, catheter, tape, tourniquet, and pre-filled syringes (out of the room till needed).

THE LAST VISIT

Having the equipment discreetly to hand means more efficiency.

If the patient is small, move the table so that there is room all around it. Place chairs on both sides so clients can sit at the table and can fuss and comfort their pet comfortably. Place sheets on the table and soft bedding on top.

Again, place a box of tissues on the corner of the table.

Spray the bedding with an herbal remedy or a pheromone spray to help to reduce stress.

Turn off the telephone in that room, there is nothing worse than someone calling the wrong extension by mistake.

THE LAST VISIT

Have voile drawstring bags available for fur clippings. Ask the client if they want a fur clipping or even a paw print.
Voile bags look so much nicer than a clear zip lock bag.

Have a roll of paper towel handy to discretely dispose of any urine or faeces.

Allow the client a few uninterrupted moments after their pet has passed.

Offer a glass of water or even a cup of tea. Phoning the client to make sure they got home ok if they were too upset to drive.

Having a box of tissues to hand is useful, but have them so they are

THE LAST VISIT

discreet. I learnt that giving tissues too soon can be a sign that the person in receipt is being told they have cried enough and this is a sign to stop.

If the client came alone, after the euthanasia escort them to their car, don't leave them to go out alone.

If you can, and if the client wishes, carry the pet to the car, ideally the client should not be expected to carry their pets body.

Be as respectful to the deceased as you would if they were alive. Treat them with dignity, love, and respect.

THE LAST VISIT

Have a trusted staff member available, someone sympathetic who is known to the client if possible. Make sure the client has details of a pet bereavement counsellor or the Blue Cross helping to ensure they have support if needed.

Make sure there is a back door that the client can leave through, so they don't have to walk back through a busy reception area.

Payment is a difficult subject to raise. Ideally the client should pay before they go into the appointment. However, it depends on the client and how long they have been at the practice. It may be possible to call or send a letter

THE LAST VISIT

in a couple of days after the consult.

I used to ask the client if they wanted to pay when they sign the consent form, I put it to them that this way we would not need to bother them afterwards, and the clients seemed happy to do this, as then they could just leave.

Can you imagine standing at the front desk, having just lost your beloved pet, and then having to sort out the money?

As a staff member, it would feel awkward, as a client it would feel embarrassing, stressful, and to some degree disgusting to even contemplate.

THE LAST VISIT

Take payment over the phone prior to the euthanasia, or send an invoice. This means that there is one less stressor for the client.

Having a payment plan in place for clients on a low income is another way to support the client. Or like the healthy clubs that some practices offer, there could be a pay as you go scheme. This allows clients to pay so much a month and ensures they have the funds to pay for the euthanasia and cremation if wanted. Sometimes clients are unable to request ashes to be returned due to financial restraints.

Sympathy cards are sent out by most practices after a euthanasia.

THE LAST VISIT

Ideally a member of staff should handwrite the card rather than use a practice stamp. Putting the names of the staff present on the day can be a nice gesture, but ideally all staff names from that branch should be on there. You can also buy packets of forget me not seeds which are a nice token.

NEVER send an invoice with the card, and try not to write the card before the client has left the building.

Ideally send it a day after the euthanasia, but no later than 2 days.

Leaving the client with their pet after the euthanasia is important if the client wishes it. We are giving them privacy to say goodbye, but the client knows we are close by when they want to leave.

Wherever possible try not to leave the pet in the room alone when the owner goes to leave. Have someone stay with the pet, stroking them, or covering them with a blanket. This is done while another person takes the client to an exit which is ideally *not* through the reception area.

There is no call for allowing a grieving client to walk through a busy waiting room, with either an empty lead or empty hands. This is not only upsetting for the client, but makes it uncomfortable for all the other clients in the waiting room. However, this being said I understand that not all clinics have the space to allow this.

There are going to be sometimes when you are asked to let a client view their pets body. When a pet is brought in after an accident or has been found in a bad way and had already died.

There are occasions when the client has only just found out about their pet after days, and the pet has been in cold storage.

There are things we can do to make the viewing a little easier for the client.

Obviously, the client is going to be very upset to begin with and how we present the pet for the viewing can make this experience a little less distressing. It is understood that we should make sure there is no blood or other bodily fluids on the pet. That they have any obvious wounds dressed and that they are laid on whichever side is more presentable.

There may be a need to pre-warn the client if the pet has been placed in cold storage. You do not have to go into detail about what this entails, as this is too much.

There may be occasions when the pet has been so badly injured that the client cannot view it no matter how well we dress the wounds and present the body.

THE LAST VISIT

In circumstances like this it is of great importance that the client has someone in the practice that they can talk to. This is where the bereavement counselling training comes in.

If a client is to view their pet, you may present the pet in the same way you prepare for the euthanasia.

A thick soft blanket on a vetbed is ideal. Placing incontinence sheets underneath to soak up any bodily discharge, this MUST be removed before the client enters the room. I know this seems a bit of a no brainer, but it can be overlooked in a busy surgery.

THE LAST VISIT

The bed is now ready, the pet has been cleaned where appropriate and any wounds dressed as if the pet were still alive, the dressings are there to hide any injury and must look decent.

Lay the pet in as natural position as possible, maybe resting the head on the fore paws, or as if asleep. A rolled-up towel can be useful to raise the head and make the pet look more comfortable. Lay a blanket over the pet leaving the head and neck uncovered. Have a box of tissues on the end of the table.

Before the client enters the room pre-warn them of the position of the pet, whether the pet is going to be facing them as they enter the room or not. For animals that have already passed there are few changes to be made. However, there are still subtle things we can do to make the viewing easier.

1. Placement of the patient. the patient in as natural a position as possible can be a nice touch, and means a lot to the client.

Laying the patient in sternal with its head on a rolled-up towel, paws either side. Or in lateral recumbency curled up as if asleep. Placing a blanket over the pet keeping the head uncovered.

2.   Avoiding potential leaks.

As macabre as it may sound, it may be necessary to protect against the leaking of bodily fluids.

A roll of soffban placed in the rectum can stop any faecal loss (I accept no responsibility for faecal loss if this method doesn't work).

Using a swab to clean the nostrils and another to clean the mouth and moisten the tongue so it can be placed back into the mouth if necessary.

3.   Pre -warning the client of the position of the body.

Pre-warn the client if the pet has its eyes open, if it is facing the door

THE LAST VISIT

etc. It may not seem that important but it can make all the difference. It allows the client to prepare themselves before they go in.

Believe me, this can have a major impact. When my grandad died, I went to see him in the funeral parlour. I was not warned about his position. This being the case, the first thing I saw was the row of thick black stitches in his head after his post mortem.

I was not warned about this, and there had been no attempt to hide them. This image has stayed with me for many years, and just shows that there are some things that seem trivial to some, but mean a lot to other people. No matter how well the euthanasia went, the owner may still have noticed smaller distractions or events.

Reminders for vaccinations, worming etc. should be taken off the clients account as soon as possible. This ensures that a client does not get a reminder for a booster for their pet that they have just lost.

There are few things more heart-breaking than having to listen to a client try to hold it together over the phone to tell you that they received a reminder in error.

Chapter 5.

How the client can help in the last days.

Receiving a poor or grave prognosis is one of the most traumatising events in our lives. Hearing that our beloved pet is seriously or terminally ill is devastating.

There are so many emotions, so much to take in. The client is more than likely thinking of anything that they can possibly do to help. The client may have been thrown a lifeline that means that they can extend the life of their pet, and even if just for a short period, they will take any chance.

Obviously, we must be realistic, and ensure that the client is aware that this is palliative care, it is not a cure, the result will be the same, although we may have bought some time. The client may be feeling lost, helpless, and scared.

We as veterinary staff can provide a gold standard of support here, as we do and must do all through the pet's life. We can provide support for the client, so that they can feel as prepared as possible for the end, but also feel that they have truly done all they humanly could. We know how to feed and medicate pets, whether they are ill or recumbent through injury. We can assist the clients by passing on our knowledge and tips to make the process easier.

Decrease in appetite or anorexia may be due to a decreased sense of smell or taste. Think back to a time when you were ill, or had a bad cold, and the last thing you wanted to do was eat. There are methods we can use to encourage patients to eat. Pour beef or chicken stock over food for extra odour.

Warm the food up to body temperature which makes it more appetising than cold food. Try not to overload the patient with food choices.

A mistake I used to make with inappetant patients was to have 3 or 4 dishes in front of them, hoping they would opt for something.

What I learned I was doing was making them feel worse. If you felt nauseous would you want someone thrusting various meals under your nose? Would it tempt you to eat?

An effect of the disease that afflicts them could cause issues with rapid weight loss and the need for an increase in nutritional intake, i.e. cancer.

"Many tumours use glucose and the rate of turnover of glucose has been estimated to be up to 80% greater in cancer patients than in normal patients. Glucose is an essential energy source for several organs, including the brain, so if the animal does not compensate by eating more food, it has to breakdown its own body stores of energy (fats, glycogen and proteins) to maintain blood glucose concentrations." (Provet, 2013) quote from website courtesy of www.provet.co.uk.

Pain can also cause inappetence. This seems an obvious reason for not eating. It is also a potential barrier to healing, as we need food and the nutrition from feeding to enable us to heal from whatever ails us, if healing or recovery is a possibility. We need to ensure that the patient is receiving enough energy to compensate for the losses. This in turn helps them to recover if recovery is possible.

Obstructions which prevent feeding is also a factor. This could be because of a foreign body such as a mass or an object which obviously provides a physical barrier, or a collar which the pet cannot navigate so they become depressed and stop trying to eat which becomes a mental barrier.

However, we can give pain medication to alleviate discomfort, we can administer appetite stimulants. The collar can be changed to a comfy collar or even a surgical shirt can be used instead.

Side effects of the medications used to treat the ailment may cause nausea which is another factor to bear in mind, and so anti emetics may be used to counter act this.

The pain relief may cause gastro intestinal irritation so gut protectants may be prescribed.

It may be worthwhile writing down for the client what has been prescribed but also explaining on paper *why*. If the client knows what and why exactly a medicine has been prescribed, they may feel more in control. They are more likely to administer the meds rather than assuming if the patient seems better they don't need it.

A lot of the time clients may stop administering meds if the patient perks up but not realising that the patient has perked up *because* of the meds. Or not administering something because they do not understand what it is, or believe that it is beneficial.

For the client, there are some tips to encourage their pets to eat such as:

Offering a certain type or brand that the pet prefers over all others.

 Add water so that the pet can lap instead of trying to chew.

THE LAST VISIT

Make the food into small balls so it can be easily swallowed rather than chewed.

Hand feed.

Little and often meals.

If the pet is to be fed a prescription diet, introduce it as you would any new food, slowly and over a period of at least 5-10 days.

Medication and its application is also very important, and if a pet is not taking its medication this can be a source of stress for the client as they know that the pet needs the meds to keep them comfortable or to help them recover.

It may be worth bearing in mind the owner, and their abilities.

THE LAST VISIT

Can they administer a capsule or tablet orally if the pet won't eat? Can they open a normal child proof lid? Can they draw up liquids?

If the answer is no, then we need to rethink how we help the client to administer meds. Is it possible to give the patient a long acting injection?

Can the meds be put into a bottle with a normal screw on top? or a Ziploc bag?

Can liquids be drawn up into prefilled syringes?

Could multiple meds be mixed into one capsule?

There are so many things changing in both the pet's life and the client's life. To make this time easier for all concerned, try to think of the home from the pet's view.

Are there plenty of soft places for the pet to stop and rest?

Are there hiding places so the pet can escape and have some time alone?

Make sure that the furniture stays where it has always been so that the pet can navigate their way around.

If they are physically unsteady it may be worth moving objects at head height that can harm the pet.

If the patient is not likely to recover, then the least we can do is allow the client to do their best. We know why we give the meds we do, we know the potential outcomes of the condition affecting the patient.

However as mentioned in a prior chapter, we must remember that the client does not have the background we do. Therefore, we need to ensure that all parties are understanding of what needs to be done to benefit the patient.

Chapter 6.

What to say and what NOT to say.

I am a Pet Bereavement Counsellor, and I have done a lot of research into what to say, what not to say. I was guilty years ago, (when I didn't know any better) of saying the wrong thing. What I found while researching, was that there were very few articles or books that told you what to say or not to say. There was always texting to say that you should be respectful, be sympathetic etc., which is fine, but that doesn't tell you *what* to do.

There are many things to say and some things that should never be uttered.

So, what *do* you say to someone that has just lost a beloved pet? Are there always things to say for any moment?

There are some things that we say that although they are meant in a sympathetic way, they can come across as anything but.

Here are some examples of what *not* to say to a grieving person.

<u>I know how you are feeling.</u>

No, you don't. Not one bit. You have *no* idea how that person feels. You know how *you* would feel, but that isn't the same.

You have no idea what is going on in that person's life, and how the loss affects them.

It may be said to mean well, but it comes across badly. It takes something away from that person, and puts the attention on you. It invalidates the grief of that person, it makes it sound as though everyone has felt or does feel like they do now, it's not new, it's not unique, what's the big deal.

THE LAST VISIT

The whole point of consoling someone is to allow them to open to you, and express *their* grief.

<u>She or he is in a better place.</u>

Really? I can understand why people may think this is helpful, but it isn't.

On the one hand, it sounds that you are recognising that the pet is no longer suffering. It is plainly obvious that the pet is better not suffering and everyone knows that.

However, saying this comes across wrong, and can make someone even more upset. It is almost like the person doing the consoling is saying that the life the pet had was awful, and they are much better off now. I know that this isn't how this statement is intended, but that is how it can be taken.

How are you doing?

The only answer you will receive here is one that is going to shut down the conversation and lead to the bereaved person putting on a brave face. What response is expected?

How do you think the client is doing? They have lost a beloved part of their family, and things may seem bleak and depressing to them. The world has changed, and there is no up and down there is only grief.

THE LAST VISIT

The person asking this is probably
not actually interested, they are
just making conversation and
doing so awkwardly. As if they
know they should say something,
anything. The bereaved person is
going to say that they are fine,
doing ok, and have a sad smile on
their face.

It was just a (insert type of pet
here)

This is one of those sentences
uttered by people who have either
never had a pet, or never cared for
a pet. Those that feel that an
animal life is no equal to a human
one. The people that cannot
comprehend how someone could
love a pet as much as or in some

cases more than a human. This comment is not meant to be sympathetic, it is not meant to be consoling. It is a blatant disregard and disrespect of someone's pain.

To that person, the pet they lost was so much more than a 'pet', and to even say the above statement does nothing but diminish any respect that person may have had for you. This statement is not helpful in any way and cannot be taken to be anything but hurtful.

<u>You can always get another one</u>

This statement really upsets me. There are no words to describe how angry this makes me feel. You

THE LAST VISIT

would not dream of saying this to someone that had lost a human family member, so why do people think it is acceptable to say to someone that has lost a pet?

Yes, we can adopt or rescue another pet, but that doesn't mean that the pain of losing one isn't debilitating.

We can never replace the pet we lost, and this statement just serves to imply that the lost life didn't matter, that they are replaceable and disposable. It is a cruel thing to say, and should never be said.

THE LAST VISIT

<u>I don't know what I would do if my pet died.</u>

In some way, I can see why someone would say this. It is sometimes said as a way of saying that you sympathise with their loss, as you personally would find it hard to deal with. However, this is not a suitable thing to say, as it turns the attention onto you. The person grieving is then left with the difficult task of trying to suppress their grief and try to console *you.*

When I was about 12 years old a girl I went to school with had a German Shepherd called Max. He was a big lovable lump, and I grew very fond of him.

THE LAST VISIT

He was an awesome dog. One day I found out that he had died, and the girl I knew was obviously very upset.

We all did our best to console her as pre-teens can, and when we got to school she was upset in Registration. Naturally all our classmates gathered round to hear why she was so upset.

One girl commented on how upset she would be if her dog died. An innocent statement, she was just saying. However, I was annoyed, *how dare she talk about her dog that was still alive, when this girl's dog was dead.* I took her to one side and basically said that no one needed to hear how upset she would be, her dog was alive, we needed to support the girl whose dog was dead.

As you can imagine, it didn't go down very well, and I was alienated even more from my peers. But I had felt that she was taking the focus away from the other girl, that although yes it would be sad, the other girl did not need reminding that other people still had their dogs. See, I told you I didn't always know what to say.

At least it was quick

I must admit that I have said this to clients after an RTA, when they ask did they suffer. I used to say I am sure they didn't, it would have been quick. I say this because in that moment the client doesn't want to imagine their pet suffering, they do not need that imagery and those thoughts.

It is a white lie, as I do not know for certain, but I am not going to say the opposite.

For losses of any other reason, I can understand why this may seem like a good thing to say. The person saying it is saying that it was quick and so for the pet it was painless and therefore easier to deal with the loss.

However, depending on the client, this can be one of the worst things to say as it is of no consolation to the owner that the pet died quickly if the death was through illness, it is not a phrase that is going to cause anything but unintended pain.

Here are some things that you *should* say:

<u>I'm sorry for your loss.</u>

This statement is meant from the heart, it doesn't necessarily need any additional words and is supportive.

It says that you feel for the bereaved, and you are sorry that they are going through such a tough time.

THE LAST VISIT

<u>You are in my thoughts; I am thinking of you.</u>

This is such a lovely thing to say. It shows you really care for the person grieving and are genuinely caring about them.

It is a statement that can be put in a card or said and left at that without elaborating and potentially saying something rash that may undo the good. Sometimes we say too much and end up doing more harm than good, no matter how unintentional.

<u>He/she was a wonderful pet.</u>

You are complimenting and honouring the deceased pet. To the client, you are showing that their beloved pet meant something to you also. It is a lovely thing to say because you are recognising and appreciating what the client has lost. Most times this may be met with a smile and a story from happier times, lifting the client's mood even if only temporarily, but it means so much.

<u>I will miss him/her</u>

We all have known that patient, the one that snuck into your heart, the one you smile at when you see their name on the waiting list. That patient that you can't help but love even though you know you shouldn't have favourites.

THE LAST VISIT

The title phrase is a way of letting the owner know that the loss will also affect you, and that you personally will feel that there is something missing from day to day. It shows the owner that their pets passing had an impact on those that knew them, and to the owner is taken that the pet was a bit more special and meant something to others. To most owners their pet is awesome, the best in the world, and to hear others say it, and mean it, is a wonderful gift.

It shows that you are sympathetic, and that you can relate on some level to the client. You all lost someone special, the loss affects you all in your own ways.

This must be so hard for you.

By saying this, you are acknowledging the grief, and the impact the loss may be having on the person. It allows the client to let out some of their feelings. It may be that the owner has encountered those that do not 'get' the pain of the loss, those that cannot or will not understand why the loss is so painful. By acknowledging the death, you are showing that you understand, also allowing the client to talk to you, knowing they will be listened to.

THE LAST VISIT

<u>Do use the pets name.</u>

Don't be afraid to speak the name of the pet. Sometimes we may feel that it will be upsetting for the client to hear their pets name.

Often it may be that *avoiding* saying the name is more upsetting. As if the pet is forgotten.

The owner will not be offended if you say the name of the pet they lost. If anything, it can be a source of comfort that the pet is remembered.

<u>Do share your favourite memory of the pet.</u>

This is a lovely thing to do if the time seems right. It opens a

THE LAST VISIT

conversation and can allow the client to talk about their pet and relive some happier times, this gives the owner something to talk about that brings a smile and happier memories, no matter how short lived.

I have seen photographs that clients have brought in, and have commented appropriately, about how the pet looked like a right scamp, or was handsome or pretty. The owner smiles, and then they proceed to tell a tale about their pet.

You can hear in their voice and see in their face that they are happy to share, and the memory brings a smile.

Chapter 7.

Stages of grief.

The reason I named my business Cycle Counselling was because of Elisabeth Kübler-Ross.

Elisabeth Kübler-Ross was a Swiss-American psychiatrist, a pioneer in near-death studies and the author of the ground-breaking book On Death and Dying, where she first discussed her theory of the five stages of grief. (Wikipedia).

In 1969 Elisabeth Kubler Ross wrote a book called 'On death and dying', in which there are described 5 stages of grief and bereavement. However, it was never intended for these 5 stages to be a definitive guide to grief and bereavement, they are the feelings expressed by the dying. A cycle of grief to some, and so I counsel those in that cycle. Below is a copy of a letter that I sent to a client recently. This is my version of what the five stages mean and how they may manifest.

Below are the 5 stages of grief. Bear in mind that grief affects us all differently, and some people may experience every stage, or experience a stage and get 'stuck' in that stage. It is a cycle, and we may revisit each part until we reach acceptance, but we may go back at some point to an earlier part of the cycle.

Denial - This is the minds way of trying to save us from the heartache, if it didn't happen we can't get hurt. We may have told ourselves that the vet was wrong, that there must have been something else, or that what was said didn't apply to our pet.

But this stage means that you are not allowing yourself to move on, you are at risk of causing longer term pain by denying what you know to be true.

THE LAST VISIT

Painful as it is, we must accept what has happened before we can try to move on.

Anger- This may be self-directed, maybe feeling we should have done things differently, why didn't we do a, b, or c?

This may be directed at a loved one because it is sometimes easier to take out our pain and frustration on a loved one because we know they will not abandon us, and will understand. The anger may be directed at the vet, for making the diagnosis in the first place. The feelings seem irrational sometimes, but in a way, we feel that our anger at the situation gives us justification for our actions.

THE LAST VISIT

Bargaining- There may have been times when we call upon a higher power, we pray for relief, or a change in circumstances. We tell ourselves that we will do this that or the other, if only the situation we are facing changes. We do this to save ourselves, but ultimately like denial, we are only causing more pain.

We know we did all we could, and we know that there is nothing we can do to change the outcome, but by bargaining we feel that we are in control to some degree of a situation we really have no control over.

Depression- The low periods, the feeling of despair and heartache.

THE LAST VISIT

This is understandable, we have suffered a heart-breaking loss, and have been through a lot of stress. But we must remember that we did what had to be done for the sake of our beloved pet. It is natural to feel sad, to cry at the little things that remind us of what we have lost. But remember that we have responsibilities, and people and may be other pets that need us.

If there is a point where we ask what is the point, or we lose interest in day to day routine, then it may be helpful to see a G.P as the burden of the loss, can lead to a deeper depression which needs support.

THE LAST VISIT

Acceptance- We accept that there was nothing more we could have done. That our actions were only in the best interest of our pet. That we gave so much, and did all that was humanly possible.

We can look back on the memories and smile, and we may cry but we can one day think about the antics of our loved one, and the memories bring a smile not pain.

There is no fixed rule to grieving, everyone deals with it in their own way, in their own time.

There is no time limit to grief. And there is no shame in having good days, or days when we may not have our lost one on our minds.

There is no shame in allowing another pet into our lives, we can never replace the pet we lost, but we can replace the normality of having a pet in the house. There is nothing to say that we must wait. Nor is there anything which says that we must take on another pet at all.

The message here is that you do what you need to do to get through. But do not punish yourself, do not cause harm to yourself or others. Your loved one would not want that, and it is only prolonging the recovery.

Be kind to yourself, you have lost a member of the family, so grieve, let it out. But in remembering the dead, don't forget to keep on living.

The clients we see have issues outside of the clinic that we do not know about. We cannot even begin to imagine what may be happening in their lives and so we should be careful. There will or may be times when a client may seem to be difficult, blaming us or putting their anger onto us to give a justification for their actions.

As veterinary staff, we book in appointments, and see and treat animals, but we have no idea what happens outside of the surgery.

THE LAST VISIT

The point I am trying to make is that not everything is as it seems.

We sometimes may make a snap judgement and react accordingly, but we should do a bit of detective work.

Trying to think about *why* a client behaves the way they do at a given moment, and not just focussing on the behaviour.

For instance, a client has had their beloved pet put to sleep, and they are angry about the costs involved.

The owner may be ranting and raving and accusing the practice of just 'being in it for the money'.

Now I used to take this personally, it felt like an attack. However, I tried to think of it from the side of the client. They may be genuinely upset about the costs, but on the other hand fear can make people react badly.

If you have ever been in debt or struggling for money, then you will know how it seems that everything costs a lot more than you think it should (in this mindset anyway).

When you get an unexpected bill, and cannot see a way to pay it fear can turn to anger.

It is a way of releasing the anxiety that the debt can bring. The client may react in an angry manner because this means that they feel justified in their actions, and they have some control over an area of their life that seems out of control.

The important thing to remember here is that the anger is not necessarily directed at you or the practice.

They have just lost their pet, and now they have a large bill, and they want cremation and the ashes back but they know they cannot afford to pay.

This is where the feelings of anger and loss of control come in. It is a possible scenario and therefore we can react accordingly.

We can take the client to a quiet room away from an audience, we can speak to them about the costs.

Breaking down the invoice so the client knows exactly why the cost is as it is. We can also speak to the practice manager or Clinical Director and try to organise a payment plan. Doing so can help to relieve some of the tension experienced.

We cannot bend the rules of the practice, we cannot cut costs just because someone is angry. What we can do though, is try to reach a mutually agreeable decision.

The reception staff are the ones who are more likely to experience the full brunt of the emotions the client is experiencing. Grief makes us react in unpredictable ways, but it also makes us desperate to change what we know we cannot.

Bargaining.

The owner may try to strike up a deal with the vet or other members of staff. They may ask for options that are unrealistic or may not listen to what has been said.

This is mainly since they have received bad news, a poor prognosis, and therefore they want to do anything they can to change the outcome. There is no point in trying to agree with the client, and there is no positive outcome from trying to appease the client by creating an option that they know will not change the outcome. Be firm in what has been said, do not change what has been said, so as not to give the client false hope.

Denial.

The client is unable to or unwilling to believe what has been said. The client may not be willing to listen to any words of comfort no matter how well intended. They may have received a poor prognosis, or the pet has passed and the vet has confirmed this.

The brain refusing to process the information, a way of protecting us from the news. This client needs to be listened to, although more than

likely they will not listen when
spoken to.

Chapter 8.

Types of grief and their meanings.

Anticipatory Grief- This type of grief is experienced when we are informed of an impending loss, whether it be a loss of life (our own or someone close to us) or the loss of something that means our lives are changed irrevocably.

Normal Grief- This type of grief is the term given to the emotions, physical and psychological, cognitive manifestations that occur upon suffering a bereavement, or a loss of something that is of great importance to us.

Complicated Grief- This type of grief is made up of different types of grief such as Chronic grief, delayed grief, masked grief, and exaggerated grief.

Chronic grief is described as the normal grief reactions that one would expect after a bereavement of some kind, but the person suffering from chronic grief tends to experience these reactions far longer than expected.

Delayed grief is when a person has suffered a traumatic loss and is unable to deal with the pain consciously or subconsciously blocks or prolongs grieving so as not to feel the emotional pain which is associated with the loss.

Exaggerated grief is when a survivor of a loss decides that the loss is too great, and they may end their own lives as they do not see the point in living without the lost loved one.

Masked grief is the term used for a person that may be displaying behaviours that are causing harm to themselves or others around them and they are not aware that these behaviours stem from the loss they have suffered.

THE LAST VISIT

Complicated grief, as the name suggests is the name given to a person who has suffered a loss through a particularly traumatic way, they may have lost several loved ones, or they may have other losses that they had not fully deal with.

So, the unresolved grief comes to the surface and makes the current loss harder to bear. There may be a lack of support from family and friends, or there may be underlying mental issues that may cause the bereaved to have difficulty coping.

Disenfranchised Grief- There are many reasons as to why a person may be experiencing this type of grief. There are losses that we suffer that cannot be expressed aloud, or are frowned upon or just generally not understood.

There are some losses that may make people wonder why the bereaved is so upset, and that person can feel alienated as though their feelings are not valid. In this case society tends to dictate what is an 'acceptable' loss to grieve for.

Therefore, people apologise before expressing their feelings. They anticipate the reaction because so often people do not think of losing a pet as on a par with losing a family member for example. However, to a lot of people, their pets _are_ like family members.

THE LAST VISIT

The loss of a pet can have a deeper impact than we may be aware of. There are many ways that a pet may leave us, and there is no telling what other issues are going on in private.

For example, a person has a pet that belonged to a late relative, the pet dies and the person must deal with any unresolved loss that stems from the loss of the relative. As far as they can see it is like losing the loved one all over again.

That pet was the last living link.

Maybe the person feels guilty, because they never liked the pet but felt obligated to rehome it.

THE LAST VISIT

Maybe now it has died or become gravely ill and they feel bad because of their feelings towards the pet.

The pet could have been an assistance animal. A Guide Dog, a therapy animal, or medical detection dog. The loss is felt more keenly because that animal was not just a pet, they were almost like an extension of that person, giving them their independence.

Then when they lose that pet there is so much more to deal with than the death. There may be feelings of guilt associated with making the decision for euthanasia.

Without prior discussion or advice, the owner can sometimes feel pressured into making the decision.

There isn't enough time it seems and suddenly, the decision to end the pet's life must be made there and then.

Chapter 9.

Grief in surviving pets.

Whether pets grieve for a lost companion is open to opinion.

Some people feel that the pets left in the household do grieve as humans do. That they pine for their lost companion and suffer a type of depression as it were.

Some owners report that their remaining pets vocalise, go off their food or become otherwise depressed.

In cases where the pets are social animals such as dogs or guinea pigs or other small furries, there may be a change in behaviour.

This may be due to the sudden disappearance of their companion and in prey animals especially, this could cause anxiety, as the cause of the disappearance is not known.

Allowing the remaining pet (if circumstances allow) to view the body of the deceased. This means that the pet can smell the body and maybe try to provoke a response.

This way hopefully it seen that the remaining pet realises that their companion has passed away.

There is some debate as to whether this is anthropomorphising (attributing human behaviours) but again this is personal.

There may be changes in the pet's behaviour, this may be due to change in routine or due to the absence of their companion.

Provide as much attention as possible and feasible, and try to keep the routine as normal as possible if this is agreeable with the surviving pet.

If the client reports that their pet is acting strangely, it may be worth asking for a check up to rule out any physical causes such as illness the signs of which may be masked.

THE LAST VISIT

If this has been ruled out, then it may be best for the pet to be treated as if it were grieving, and treat accordingly.

When burying a pet in the garden it is advised that any other pets are not aware of the burial site in case they return to exhume the body.

Chapter 10.

How to help staff.

Day in day out we as veterinary staff see things that give us a smile, a laugh, and a shake of the head.

Some days we see puppies and kittens and young and old pets. We see the happy owners, the sad owners the angry owners.

We see some things that we may happily tell our families about, and we see some things that keep us awake at night. Some things that make us so sad, and make us hug our fur babies a bit tighter.

There are bound to be some cases that never leave you. Some cases of abuse or neglect. Those cases that make you wonder how you can go on in the profession.

There may have been a day that seemed to be filled with euthanasia's which can take a lot out of someone.

Team work is what makes these days more bearable. As a team, you can get through all this, and still look forward to the next day's work.

THE LAST VISIT

There are things you can do as a practice to make the working life easier when times are stressful.

There have been many times when staff work through dinner, not stopping to eat at all. There isn't enough time, there are 101 things to do. At the practice I used to work at the Clinical Director would order pizza when we were all rushed off our feet.

When we had hardly time to breathe. It was a welcome treat, and easy to grab a slice on the way to the next job on the never-ending list.

Baking: some staff bake cakes, and a couple of times a week there may be homemade goodies to help yourself to. Why not ask staff to bake or bring in cakes or chocolates now and again?

A team night out, this can be a night on the town, or a night at the cinema, or Bingo even. It's just a night where the staff can let their hair down and have a laugh.

These ideas are not new, and you may already have a similar team building event. But by having fun together, it can strengthen the bond in the workplace.

THE LAST VISIT

There can be divides between staff types, the vets and vet nurses, the auxiliaries, and the reception team etc.

But we are all in this profession for the same reason. We want to help animals and we want to help the people that care for those animals.

So, we must not forget this. We should respect rank as it were, but also respect that we are all dedicating our time to animals.
We must also place ourselves in our colleague's shoes.
Has anyone ever asked the reception team if they are ok after a client has been screaming at them. Has anyone taken over for a

minute so the receptionist can have a minute?

Has anyone ever spoken to the vet that performed several euthanasia's or has performed a traumatic operation?

With regards to vets and euthanasia, we can sometimes take for granted that they are ok, that its part of their job. However, I don't think that the actual decision making and procedure is ever easy. And no matter how many times it is done I would imagine that it gets harder. That there are those cases that must prey on their mind.

At one of my first CPD's that I tutor, we had a vet attend.

I brought up the subject of support among staff, and suggested that we don't always tend to think about the vet. This lady shook her head sadly and it was clear that just because it is in your job role, does not make it easier to do.

We need to delegate more, enlist support from team members instead of trying to do it all and to no avail.

We need to praise the staff that try hard, and stop letting the staff that do nothing get away with it.

We all have that one member, the one who does nothing yet gets away with it, no repercussions. And we have the ones who do all the work and get no recognition.

This must stop.

THE LAST VISIT

Monthly meetings can be held and the staff are encouraged to write down items for discussion. A board could be set aside for staff to bring up any issues that bother them, the head nurse and Clinical Director or Practice Manager can look at these and address them. It is important that any issues raised are dealt with, as it can destroy morale if it seems that your voice is never heard.

Staff need to know that they are a valued member of the team.

We need to make sure that everyone pulls their weight, or else the team can become fragile and demoralised.

THE LAST VISIT

What's the point in doing your best when no one seems to notice?

Make sure that you tell someone that they are doing a good job, tell them one good thing they have done that day. All too often there are those staff members that are always told what they are doing wrong, and never or rarely told what they are doing right.

Take a minute to discuss possible reasons for loss of team morale.

What is happening between staff? Are all members of the team mentally and physically ok?

Having a quiet room can be useful. A spare room filled with bean bags, pillows, music, and soft lighting.

THE LAST VISIT

Somewhere where staff can have a moment.

A place to have a breather, a place to gather their thoughts or scream into a cushion.

Make sure all staff are aware of support within the practice, whether it is a helpline number, or a counsellor in practice. Even just having a mental health meeting to discuss any issues staff may have, and work together to create a healthier happier workplace.

Remember that we have NO idea what goes on in someone's life outside of work. Many people try to leave home issues there, and work issues at work.

THE LAST VISIT

But this doesn't always happen. What we find easy to deal with may be the last straw for someone else.

Care for yourself and your colleagues.

There are too many things we see that cause upset, and sometimes there is no one we can talk to that will understand. *Talk to each other, support each other, and make sure you all pull your weight.*

Chapter 11.

Other sources of support.

If you are struggling to help the client further, you can always suggest the following.

Cycle Counselling

A pet bereavement Service run by myself (Carrie Ball) a Veterinary Care Assistant with over 16 years' experience.

07522202498

Cyclecounselling@hotmail.com

@cyclecounselling on Facebook

THE LAST VISIT

Twitter: @cballpetlosscounsellor

Compassion Understood UK.

A wonderful site that provides support in the form of online training for staff, and information sheets for clients.
info@compassionunderstood.com

The Ralph Site.

A website that has a list of Pet Bereavement Counsellors. It also has information available for clients.

They also have a page on Facebook which is a group that offers support to owners. The support group is an invaluable source of support. The people that comment are all pet owner's past or present, the group is very supportive. www.theralphsite.com

https:/m.facebook.com.TheRalphSite

The Blue Cross Pet Bereavement Support Service

A free helpline run by trained volunteers, who are or were pet owners.

www.bluecross.org 0800

096 6606.

For Children:

There are a few books available for varying ages. They explain death and loss in a way that enables parents and children to discuss the topic, and learn how to cope.

Books.

Megan's Journey by

Janet Peel.

A personal favourite of mine. The illustrations are beautiful, and the story can be read by a child and understood, or it can be read to a child. Adults and children have all said it is a very helpful book.

Goodbye Mousie

by Robie H Harris.

THE LAST VISIT

Losing my pet

By Alex Lambert (6yrs

old).

Phone and web help.

ChildLine

ChildLine are there for young children to talk to.

There is someone on the other end of the phone who is neutral, and the child may feel better talking to someone they do not know. It is sometimes easier to say everything you want to say to a relative stranger.   0800 1111
www.Childline.org.uk

THE LAST VISIT

This book was written to compliment a CPD accredited course tutored by myself brought to you by Innovet-CPD Training. The book does not replace the course, nor does the course replace the book.

Innovet-CPD Training

 www.innovet-cpd.co.uk

Innovet CPD Training is a Veterinary CPD provider

 'Established in 2008, InnoVet CPD Training is a leading training company providing quality Accredited CPD training within the Veterinary sector'.

This is a one-day course, worth 7 hours of CPD and is Accredited.

THE LAST VISIT

Modules

1: The Human-Animal Bond

· Different Types of Bond

· Respecting Spiritual Beliefs and Values

·Emotional and Psychological Aspects of Losing a Pet

2: The Bereavement Process

· Stages of Grief

· The Loss of Assistance Animals

· Grief in Surviving Pets

· Children and Pet Loss

· The Elderly and Pet Loss

THE LAST VISIT

·   Client Bereavement Support Materials

I have felt for many years that there needs to be more support for clients in veterinary practice. Luckily times are and have changed a lot. If we cannot provide some level of support and understanding, then the client may feel they have no one. We **can** make a difference.

Thank you for buying this book.

I would be very grateful for feedback at cyclecounselling@hotmail.com.

THE LAST VISIT

I read a good little sign once.

It said:

'If you like what we do, tell others.
If you don't, tell us'.

THE LAST VISIT

Notes

THE LAST VISIT

Notes

THE LAST VISIT

THE LAST VISIT

THE LAST VISIT

THE LAST VISIT

THE LAST VISIT

THE LAST VISIT

THE LAST VISIT

THE LAST VISIT

THE LAST VISIT

27337840R00116

Printed in Great Britain
by Amazon